IT'S TIME TO LEARN ABOUT ABOUT DEINONYCHUSES

It's Time to Learn about Deinonychuses

Walter the Educator

Silent King Books
A WhichHead Entertainment Imprint

Copyright © 2025 by Walter the Educator

All rights reserved. No part of this book may be reproduced in any manner whatsoever without written permission except in the case of brief quotations embodied in critical articles and reviews.

First Printing, 2025

Disclaimer

This book is a literary work; the story is not about specific persons, locations, situations, and/or circumstances unless mentioned in a historical context. Any resemblance to real persons, locations, situations, and/or circumstances is coincidental. This book is for entertainment and informational purposes only. The author and publisher offer this information without warranties expressed or implied. No matter the grounds, neither the author nor the publisher will be accountable for any losses, injuries, or other damages caused by the reader's use of this book. The use of this book acknowledges an understanding and acceptance of this disclaimer.

It's Time to Learn about Deinonychuses is a collectible early learning book by Walter the Educator suitable for all ages belonging to Walter the Educator's Collectible Early Learning Book Series. Collect more books at WaltertheEducator.com

USE THE EXTRA SPACE TO TAKE NOTES AND DOCUMENT YOUR MEMORIES

DEINONYCHUSES

Long ago in days gone by,

It's Time to Learn about
Deinonychuses

When dinos ruled beneath the sky,

A clever hunter roamed the land

Deinonychus, fierce and grand.

It wasn't big like some you've seen,

Just ten feet long, fast and lean.

With feathers sprouting on its skin,

It dashed through forests, slim and thin.

Its name means "terrible claw,"

A scary foot that dropped your jaw!

Each back foot had a curving hook,

One look was all it ever took.

That claw was sharp and shaped like a sickle,

Used for slashing, not a tickle!

It jumped and pounced with legs so strong,

And grabbed its prey before too long.

It's Time to Learn about
Deinonychuses

It hunted in a clever pack,

Sneaking up and then attack!

Working together to take down prey,

Like a team game they'd often play.

Its teeth were sharp, its eyes were keen,

Among the smartest ever seen.

Its brain was big for dino kind,

A thinking hunter with a plan in mind.

Though scary-sounding, it was small,

Compared to giants, not so tall.

But speed and smarts made it elite,

With claws like knives on every feet.

Some scientists think it had soft feathers,

To help it stay warm in all kinds of weathers.

It couldn't fly, but it could leap,

And race through forests, wide and deep.

Deinonychus lived in early Cretaceous,

In places now dry, once quite spacious.

Fossils found beneath the dirt,

Tell stories in each bone and skirt.

It's Time to Learn about
Deinonychuses

So if you dream of dinos wild,

Think of this one, fast and styled.

A raptor smart and full of might

Deinonychus, a real delight!

ABOUT THE CREATOR

Walter the Educator is one of the pseudonyms for Walter Anderson. Formally educated in Chemistry, Business, and Education, he is an educator, an author, a diverse entrepreneur, and he is the son of a disabled war veteran. "Walter the Educator" shares his time between educating and creating. He holds interests and owns several creative projects that entertain, enlighten, enhance, and educate, hoping to inspire and motivate you. Follow, find new works, and stay up to date with Walter the Educator™ at WaltertheEducator.com